Managing Your Classroom

D1037828

Also available in the Classmates series:

Managing Your Classroom

Gererd Dixie

continuum
LONDON • NEW YORK

Continuum

The Tower Building
11 York Road
London SE1 7NX
www.continuumbooks.com

15 East 26th Street
New York
NY 10010

First published 2003

British Library Cataloguing-in-Publication Data
A catalogue record for this book is available from the British Library.

ISBN 0-8264-6475-0

Typeset by Originator Publishing Services, Gt Yarmouth
Printed in Great Britain by Biddles Ltd, Guildford and King's Lynn

Contents

Series Introduction

Dear Teacher

Classmates is an exciting and innovative new series developed by Continuum, and is designed to help you improve your teaching and your career.

With your huge workload, both inside and outside of school, we understand that you have less time to read around your profession. These short, pithy guides have been designed with an accessible layout so that you do not have to wade through lots of dull, heavy text to find the information you need.

All of our authors have first-hand teaching experience and have written this essential series with busy teachers in mind. Our subjects range from taking school trips (*Tips for Trips*) and dealing with parents (*Involving Parents*) to coping with the large amounts of stress in your life (*Stress Busting*) and creating more personal time for yourself (*Every Minute Counts*).

If you have practical advice that you would like to share with your fellow teachers and think that you could write a book for this series, then we would be delighted to hear from you.

We do hope that you enjoy reading our Classmates. With very best wishes

Continuum's Education Team

P.S. Watch out for our second batch of ten Classmates, to be launched in March 2004

Introduction

Teachers very rarely get the chance to sit back and think about what their job is all about. In the 30 years that I have been teaching, it is fair to say that I have had very little time or space to reflect in any depth on the diverse nature of my role as a teacher. The process of carrying out academic research for my degrees and for writing this has provided me with opportunities to do just this and has allowed me to think about a whole range of issues related to my job. One of these issues forms the basis of this publication, in which I intend to focus entirely on what Zimpher and Howey (1987: 104) refer to as a teacher's technical competence in the classroom. In other words, I want to concentrate on what experienced teachers refer to as 'tactical control'.

Tactical control involves a teacher adopting a pragmatic and systematic approach to classroom management and setting up an infrastructure whereby pupil indiscipline and poor behaviour are less likely to occur. There is a whole range of practical things teachers can do to prevent indiscipline among their pupils and to facilitate real learning, which are explored here.

Guidance will, therefore, be offered in response to the following questions:

Managing Your Classroom

◆ Why is the 'establishment' phase so important to class control and discipline?

◆ Why is body language such an important aspect of class control?

◆ How can questioning be used as an effective classroom management tool?

◆ What is the role of tension in helping to establish good class control?

◆ How important is the physical environment of the classroom in establishing effective class control?

I also intend to focus on those aspects of classroom management that help to prevent pupil indiscipline from happening in the first place. I like to call it 'control by anticipation'. In other words, anticipate what could possibly go wrong in a lesson and plan for it.

What exactly do I mean by the term 'class control'? For the purposes of these pages it is viewed as:

◆ Being able to command the full attention of the pupils in the class when and where you require it.

◆ Having confidence that in free learning situations, your authority will not be diminished.

◆ Being able to maintain good informal relations with the pupils within the class, yet still maintain the ability to revert to a more controlled, formal situation whenever necessary.

Who exactly is this publication for? Primarily it is aimed at those teachers who are in the dawn of their careers – ITT (Initial Teacher Training) students, NQTs (newly qualified teachers) and teachers with one or two years' experience. However, I would strongly suggest that what I have got to say is relevant to teachers of all ages and experience. It certainly does no harm.

'NQTs express their amazement and bewilderment as to how effortlessly these experienced teachers appear to control the pupils in their classes.'

1

The Establishment Phase

What is the establishment phase and why is it important?

As part of the induction scheme in the school that I work, NQTs are given the opportunity to observe more experienced colleagues at work in the classroom. During the subsequent observation-feedback meetings, many of these NQTs express their amazement and bewilderment as to how effortlessly these experienced teachers appear to control the pupils in their classes. Being quite inexperienced in the field of reflective practice themselves, they struggle to articulate exactly what it is that allows these teachers to maintain a calm, purposeful working atmosphere in their classes, sometimes with the very same pupils they are having problems with!

Some of the NQTs put this down to the high status of the teacher being observed but were at a loss to explain the success of those experienced but low status members of staff. Others put the control down to the charismatic nature of the teacher under scrutiny. While I agree that the charisma of the teacher can often play a significant role in controlling and motivating pupils, I am convinced that, on its own, it is not enough to maintain good discipline and a well-oiled classroom machine on a consistent basis.

Throughout my career I have witnessed some very senior and charismatic staff struggling to control their classes efficiently and effectively. These teachers have become over-reliant on their personal competence to get them through their school day, instead of looking at the issue of classroom management in a broader and more balanced way. Something more is needed! So exactly what is this missing ingredient? Well, it's not rocket science! It's all down to the way that these teachers have established their rules and routines with their classes in the initial stages of the year. This socialization process is called the 'establishment phase' and its implementation is a vital ingredient of effective teaching and learning. Whether you are a student, an NQT, or an experienced teacher, planning for the establishment phase should occur well before you meet your first class.

Why is that first meeting with your class so important?

No matter how experienced a teacher is, when they stand up in front of a class for the first time, a culture of learning and behaviour is being established for the rest of the working relationship. Wragg (1995: 115) writes about the need for teachers to be skilled in the area of impression management. Goffman, (1971) cited in Wragg (1995: 115), describes the process of impression management which commences at first meetings and continues through subsequent encounters:

The individual's initial projection commits him to what he is proposing to be and requires him to drop all pretences of being other things. As the interaction among the participants progresses, additions and modifications in this informational state will, of course, occur, but it is essential that these later developments be related without contradiction to, and even built up from the initial positions taken up by several participants.

(Wragg, 1995: 115)

So what does this mean in practical terms? It is important for teachers of all ages and experience to be clear about exactly who they are, what they believe in and what they expect from their pupils. Consistency in the way you present yourself to the pupils is important at least until you become fully established with your classes. Perhaps then you can deviate slightly when you deem necessary.

This reflective process may prompt you to ask yourself some pretty searching questions about your personality and teaching behaviours. Are you arrogant, pompous, sarcastic, conceited, insensitive, dogmatic, over fussy, bad-tempered, inflexible or inconsistent? You may also have to be quite soul-searching when it comes to analysing your teaching behaviours. For example:

♦ Do you enter the room in a confident, purposeful and assertive manner?

♦ Do you use assertive body language when speaking to the pupils? (Head up, chin tilted slightly forward, shoulders back and easy, confident pose.)

♦ Do you avoid constant hesitations such as 'er', 'um', etc.?

Managing Your Classroom

- Do you use an assertive and decisive tone of voice, changing pitch of your voice to stimulate interest in what you are saying?

- Do you stand in full view of the class to allow yourself the opportunity to scan the group?

- Do you make full eye contact with your pupils in order to (a) personally engage them in the lesson, and (b) make sure that they are on task and not messing about?

- Do you avoid making too many hand and body movements? (This tends to distract pupils' attention from what you are actually saying.)

- Do you smile at the pupils?

- Do you have annoying characteristics, such as fiddling with your hair, rolling your hands around inside your trousers, etc.?

- Do you give the impression you know what you are talking about?

- Are you boring?

I'll never cease to be amazed at how quickly individuals make up their minds about other people. As a sociology teacher I have always been very interested in the process of 'labelling' in schools. Much of my reading has focused on the labelling of pupils carried out by their teachers. However, it is equally important to explore the ways in which pupils impose labels on their teachers. In a recent discussion with my Year Eleven class, I asked the pupils about the length of time it takes for them to draw firm conclusions about their new teachers. Their response was staggering! The majority of pupils in these classes gave a new teacher between 3 and 10 minutes to prove themselves. When asked whether they were prepared to re-negotiate these initial impressions, very few of them admitted to changing their minds about their teachers in any significant way. Although this evidence is purely anecdotal you will, nevertheless, appreciate how important it is to make a positive impression on your pupils early on.

If you stay in the same school for any length of time you will certainly find the establishment phase far easier to cope with. The reputations of well-established teachers often precede them, so it is worth putting in a lot of work into this process in your early years at the school. If you move to another school, however, do not expect the transition to be smooth. Wragg (1995: 115) describes how even experienced teachers express their surprise about how difficult it is to establish their routines, rules and authority in their new schools. We need to have sympathy with supply teachers who experience numerous 'first encounters' with pupils throughout the course of their working lives. These are often traumatic experiences that many of them would wish to forget. I agree with Wragg's view that this is a very personal time for teachers and I am not surprised at his assertion that there has been so little research into these extremely intimate first moments between teacher and pupil.

I have long held the belief that the degree to which teachers are able to understand and control their

'The reputations of well-established teachers often precede them.'

emotions during these early encounters with their classes, can have a correlation with the quality of relationships with their pupils. This can have a direct consequence on the quality of their class control and discipline. With this view in mind I asked a number of teachers with varying degrees of experience to describe how they felt before they encountered their first classes at the beginning of the academic year. A selection of these responses have been included below. This next response comes from a very competent Head of Department of six years experience who writes extremely honestly about her feelings before she meets her classes for the first time.

I am always very apprehensive at the start of the term in September, with butterflies not being unusual. I have a feeling of fear that my classes will not be controllable, that I will have to struggle with them for the whole year. This never happens, but it does motivate me to ensure that my lessons incorporate as many routines as possible. I try to put emphasis on routines and standards as the main priority of the lessons, rather than content, to ensure that they (and I) know where we stand.

Readers may also be surprised to read this next response which comes from a very capable and highly respected assistant Head of Department of 24 years' experience:

The night before we return in September I know I am going to sleep badly. I wake up every hour and get up very early even though I know I have got everything ready the night before. I have to force myself to eat and drink as I always feel sick. Once I am at school I feel even more sick. When my classes arrive my mouth goes dry – I never sit down for the first lessons, I suppose I need to look more menacing and, as I am only small, standing when they are sitting, seems to make a difference. I go over what they do when arriving to the lesson, what equipment I expect them to have and my expectations of how they should behave etc. I try to get them to give me reasons for rules and I probably talk for too long! I've had nightmares about arriving a day late for school and about my classes having no teacher for that first day! The end of the first day and I am truly exhausted. I've used up my nervous energy for the next month in one go.

Students and NQTs can take heart from this next response which comes from an extremely efficient and well-respected senior teacher with 25 years' experience who was, nevertheless, still prepared to expose her vulnerabilities in writing.

I always feel really nervous before the first day in September. I never sleep well the night before and I don't feel confident when the day arrives (after 25 years). I always try to stand in the foyer early in the morning to meet the students as they arrive just to get into the swing of things! When I meet my classes for the first time I feel nervous and unsure of myself. I always go through my routines and what is expected of them but I always try to get a bit of maths in there too – so that I get to know their names as soon as possible. Something they can succeed at – nothing too difficult – so that they can go away looking forward to coming back.

The final contribution comes from a highly experienced and well thought of senior teacher to whom countless numbers of staff turn to for advice and guidance on pastoral issues in the school.

Taking a new class is always a slightly worrying experience even after all these years! 'Here we go again!' A time to make sure they know who I am and what I stand for. I never fully relax with a form until I'm sure I can do so. So many times in the past if you let them go too early, you realise you have misjudged the extent to which they've got the point. Obviously depending on the group this can take a long time – but believe it will happen. Just before I meet a new class I feel anxious (still!). Routines start day one and need constant reinforcing.

So exactly what should beginning teachers glean from these responses? First, it is important to admit to your vulnerabilities. You will have noted that staff who appear to others to be highly confident and 'in control' do not necessarily feel like that on the 'inside'. It is very much to their credit, therefore, that they have been prepared to share their feelings. I would strongly advise you to share your experiences, fears and vulnerabilities either formally with your induction tutor and/or informally with colleagues. By doing this you will begin to realize that you are not on your own and hopefully, you will begin to feel less isolated.

However, understanding your emotions is simply not enough on its own. The one thing in common among all of these respondents was that, despite having these feelings of inadequacy and insecurity, they managed to get to grips with them knowing that failure to do so would result in a breakdown in their classroom control and discipline. They were experienced enough to understand that these emotions can be controlled and that they are temporary, at least until the next cohort of pupils arrive in the following September. It is worth really steeling yourself, remaining strong and trying hard to 'bluff it out'.

So what should you do when you meet your new classes? Certainly you need to start the year off as you mean to go on. Maintain positive body language and a confident tone of voice and state your expectations

'Maintain positive body language and a confident tone of voice and state your expectations clearly and assertively to the pupils.'

clearly and assertively to the pupils. We shall discuss these issues in more detail later in Section 2. It is also very important not simply to go into the classroom and issue the pupils with a list of expectations without giving them the rationale behind your demands. Try to get across the notion that teaching and learning is very much a partnership and that both parties have to 'give and take' if they are going to be successful. Discuss the notion of 'rights' and 'responsibilities'.

I have provided a 'rights and responsibilities' contract that I use with my classes on pages 17–18, which I show to the pupils as an overhead transparency sheet before they place their signed copies into the their log books. It is very important that this contract is revisited on a regular basis throughout the academic year.

Having extolled the virtue of a working partnership with the pupils I need to make the point that the teacher should, nevertheless, be the one in control of the learning/teaching situation. In my opinion it is important for teachers and pupils to accept the following principles:

♦ The teacher should decide where pupils sit

♦ The teacher should know pupils by name

♦ The pupils should give their full attention when required

♦ The pupils should realize that any level of disruption is unacceptable

♦ There should be mutual respect between staff and pupils

♦ Each pupil should feel valued and fully involved in the learning process.

In order to achieve this it is important to set up rules and routines.

Why are clear rules and routines important to pupils?

Contemporary literature on the functions of how the brain works describe how the lower part of the brain – the reptilian brain – is in charge of the survival functions of a human being. When threatened, this part of the brain takes over. The reptilian brain must be at ease if real learning is to take place. One of the hindrances to pupil learning is 'insecurity'. Giving clear ground rules and expectations and being fair and consistent are essential in reducing this insecurity among pupils.

Despite the overt resistance of many youngsters to rules and routines, I am convinced that there is a large part of them that subconsciously demands these boundaries and this level of structure within their lessons. Carrying out these simple measures on a consistent basis will certainly help to prevent that irritating, low-level, disruptive behaviour which is so detrimental to effective teaching and learning. It is worth spending a lot of time in thinking about the sorts of routines you will need to set up in your classes.

How clear, for example, are you in your own mind that you have well-defined routines for some/all of the following teaching scenarios:

♦ when you are taking the register;

Pupil/Teacher Contract

1. What do I expect from you?

2. I expect you to be courteous to me and to the other pupils in the class.

3. I expect your *full* attention when I ask for it. This will help you to learn.

4. I expect you to be honest about yourself and to admit when you are in the wrong. (This is all part of the learning process.)

5. I expect you to meet assignment deadlines. (This helps me to help you.)

6. I expect you to do your very best. It is very important that you are able to look back at your efforts over the year with pride.

7. I expect you to accept the following consequences of not doing the above:

   I will speak to you in private.

   If you persist then I will give you a detention.

   I will contact your Head of Year.

   I will contact your parents.

However, as learning and teaching is a 'partnership' there are certain things that you have a right to expect from me.

Pupil/Teacher Contract (continued)

What can you expect from me?

♦ You can expect me to be courteous and respectful even when I am telling you off.

♦ You can expect my full efforts in helping you to progress and/or helping you through your difficulties.

♦ You can expect me to mark your work on a regular basis and to provide you with constructive feedback.

♦ You can expect me to apologize to you or the class when I get things wrong.

♦ You can expect me to treat you fairly and consistently for misbehaviour or poor work ethic.

Signed: ....Teacher

....Pupil

♦ when pupils are working in small groups;

♦ when the class is having a discussion;

♦ when pupils are taking a test;

♦ when pupils are making presentations;

♦ when pupils enter or leave a classroom;

- when pupils are in transition from one activity to another;
- when pupils are carrying out independent work;
- when pupils are clearing up; or
- when you are giving a directed lesson in front of the class?

I have included some examples of some of my classroom routines for you to have a look at. However, remember that simply taking someone else's routines and trying to make them work for you is not always effective. You need to give the system your own identity.

When I take the register

Step 1 I count down loudly and slowly from 3 to 1. Doing this provides the pupils with a warning that I am going to expect silence pretty soon and allows them that extra couple of seconds to finish what they have to say.
Step 2 I scan the room to make sure pupils are seated and facing me at the front.
Step 3 I call the names of the individual pupils out.
Step 4 I read out school notices to the pupils.
Step 5 I allow pupils to talk quietly.

When pupils enter my classroom

Step 1 Walk into the class quietly. (It is important to be precise about your requirements – don't use a phrase like 'behave appropriately'.)

Step 2   Collect resources for the lesson off the back desks.

Step 3   Collect their exercise books from the appropriate pigeon hole.

Step 4   Sit down and get their equipment out ready for the lesson.

Step 5   Attempt the 'holding' task that may be displayed on the board.

Not only do you need to be clear about your routines and rules in these situations, but it is also absolutely vital that your pupils understand exactly what is expected of them. In the cases described above, the prime reason for carrying out these routines is so that learning can take place efficiently and as soon as possible.

Whenever I talk to NQTs, students and experienced staff about their use of routines, virtually all of them tell me that they do not write these down for the pupils. It is important not to forget that many pupils are visual rather than auditory learners. They certainly need something written down in front of them if you want to stand any chance of them learning your rules and routines. In addition to this textual version of your rules and routines, you could support this with illustrations for the classroom wall. You could, for example, also discuss these routines with the class and ask your pupils to design illustrated flow diagrams/posters for each of the above routines, similar to those in Figure 1, and put them on display in your classroom. This will give them a sense of ownership of the process, which is vital if your strategies are to succeed.

Figure 1. Some examples of rules displayed in a visual form.

I would be an absolute liar if I told you that all of my routines work to perfection. I have had some very difficult classes over the years and things have not always gone as planned. However, I have tried very hard to be consistent and have enjoyed more success with these classes than had I abandoned these routines when things initially became difficult. It is also important to anticipate that pupils will constantly test you out to see whether you 'mean business' or not. In order to cater for this situation you need to design a set of 'graduated' sanctions that support the routinization process. The pupils do need to know exactly what these sanctions are. An example of these could be:

First offence – warning
Second offence – five minute clear-up duty
Third offence – official detention
Fourth offence – contact parents.

It is vital that you check, and constantly re-check that the pupils understand your routines. Don't assume that, once you have given the pupils these, they will automatically remember them. It needs a lot of hard work on your part! In some low-level research carried out with NQTs at the end of their first year, a large number of them mentioned how they wished they had been more stringent in the implementation of their rules and routines. Some of their responses can be seen below:

'What would I change with regard to rules and routines?

Teacher A

In my NQT year I should have ... been more consistent with punishments; chased up pupils who did not hand homework in on time, made a list of late homeworks and then issued detentions for three late homeworks; penalized more rigorously perpetual disorganization, missing books and equipment; made more effort to send post-cards/letters home, praising excellent work and levels of effort; awarded more raffle tickets in Years 10–11; used games, competitions and prizes as incentives as this worked and continues to work very well; made more effort with my form to really clamp down on lateness and uniform: trainers in particular; used the red and yellow card system more consistently.

To be honest, I was so busy and concerned with good teaching that rules and routines were something I didn't consciously set out to do it was the natural or instinctive way of organising my pupils. Rules and routines are a very good way of exerting, consolidating control, but also the children need some consistency. They need guidelines,

'It is vital that you check, and constantly re-check that the pupils understand your routines.'

rules and routines in their everyday life, especially as many will not get this stability at home. But I am a strong believer that rules are meant to be broken and routines should not be cast in stone. Healthy tension can be created and used through the breaking or changing of established teaching patterns and mundane day-to-day routines. Change is definitely a good way to keep pupils on their toes and leaving them excited or intrigued as to what to expect. Routines have their place but no-one should get stuck in a rut. If you are bored with it – you can guarantee the pupils will be.

Teacher B

Rules and routines are like a spine – every lesson needs a backbone.

Teacher C

At the beginning of my NQT year I was very hung up on making the right impression and making sure pupils knew I was in total control. So . . . over the summer, I wrote out my classroom rules as instructed at college. September came and I introduced each class to the 10 golden rules. This was great in theory, but in practice 10 were far too many and pupils did not remember them all. This summer I wrote my classroom rules again. There are now three, simple, straightforward statements that all pupils can understand and remember.

I was much more 'hung up' on rules last year. I expected all pupils to behave perfectly. As I have gained in experience and confidence, I've learnt that there are some pupils with whom rules have to be bent slightly in order to form positive, working relationships. This has taken nearly two years to develop and although it is not what the training centres tell you, I think that I am a better teacher because of it.

Written comments from two Science NQTs after their first year of teaching:

Teacher D

In my NQT year I made my rules very clear at the start of the academic year. However, I did not tend to remind the students of these rules during my lessons. I just expected them to remember them and got cross when they didn't. This year I remind the students frequently about my expectations at the start of each activity so that they know what they are to do. Last year I thought I did not have enough time to do this because I needed to get through so much information. This year I have begun to realize that reinforcing my rules actually saves time as I spend less time having to discipline pupils for 'silly' things like not putting hands up etc. It's not perfect but it's better than last year.

Teacher E

During my first week in the school I spent a lot of time going over the ground rules for my classroom. Most of the ground rules were volunteered by the pupils themselves and I made sure the reasons behind the rules were clear. After that I assumed the pupils would remember the ground rules and comply with them. However, without continued reinforcement the rules were soon forgotten and I found myself back to square one. My advice would be to make a big deal of the rules at the start of the year, and then to take every opportunity to reinforce them. For example, before the class watches a video, ask the pupils what the seating rule is, or before a group discussion, ask the class what rule will ensure that everybody will be heard.

Teacher F

I made the mistake of not outlining clear rules with my form at the start of last year and am still suffering from it. When I tried to establish my rules I came up with a list of ten. I now feel that they should probably be no more than four or five.

Managing Your Classroom

You need to know that there are some very strong teachers among this research sample. You can see from the high quality of their reflective comments that these members of staff have always been fully committed to the notion of establishing rules and routines with their classes from the very outset. What they admit to not doing was taking the time and trouble to reinforce these.

I also note with interest, and agreement, the comments made by Teachers A and B who write about the need to be flexible. The rules and routines in a classroom are there to establish good order and to facilitate learning. If this is not happening then change your routines but don't abandon them. I also mentioned earlier about the need to gain some ownership of your rules and routines. Teachers B and F wrote about imposing ten classroom rules as instructed by their college staff. By their own admission this simply didn't work and they felt the need to reduce this number to three or four. Teachers need to find their own way through this but what is important is to come up with a meaningful classroom regime that matches your personality and your teaching style. Whatever happens, the most important thing to remember is to reinforce rules on a consistent basis. Again, I would be lying if I said that it is easy to do this.

Interestingly enough, many teachers manage to maintain their rules and regulations almost up to the Christmas period but, as they get tired and run down, they tend to relax their hold on their classes. Many teachers relax their rules and routines much earlier than this. They may be three to four weeks into the academic year and, delighted that the expected bout

'Change your routines
but don't abandon
them.'

of indiscipline has not yet manifested itself, they start to relax and reduce their efforts as far as reinforcing the routines are concerned What they have failed to do, however, is to recognize the 'honeymoon' period that occurs with most classes after the initial three-week settling-in period. While these experienced teachers can often get away with this by re-establishing their control when they feel that things are getting out of hand, it is much more difficult for an inexperienced teacher to do this.

Teachers who are in the 'dawn of their profession' do not have this fund of reputation and experience behind them and find it a lot more difficult to claw the situation back. Teachers D and E obviously learned a very salutary lesson in their first year but now seem to have got to grips with these issues.

Obviously it is very much up to the individual as to exactly how you do this. I can only really say what works for me. For example, if I am not happy with the way the pupils have come into my lesson, I will tell them to stop what they are doing and quiz them on my expectations. With younger pupils I sometimes formalize this process by having a quick class quiz based on my classroom rules. If you have a spare minute just before the pupils leave to go to another lesson, you could use the time valuably by asking the pupils about your classroom expectations. The point of this is that, by constantly reinforcing your routines, you are socializing your pupils into your expected norms and values. As newly qualified teachers or as new teachers to a school it is worth investing a great deal of effort into socializing the younger pupils into your way of thinking. You will most certainly reap the

'The most important thing to remember is to reinforce rules on a consistent basis.'

rewards if you come across these pupils further up the school.

Giving instructions to classes

Giving instructions to pupils is not as easy as it looks. Having observed so many teachers really come unstuck when giving what they thought to be clear instructions to pupils, I am convinced that this issue needs to be given real thought. The importance of doing this is compounded if you are teaching practical lessons where pupils have a degree of freedom to use the resources located at various points in the classroom. When determining the specific instructions you want your pupils to follow, use the following guidelines:

Tips

Keep it simple!
Choose a limited number of instructions for each classroom activity.

Choose instructions that are observable.
Don't include vague instructions such as 'behave appropriately'.

Relate your instructions to:
How you want the pupils to participate in the

activity or procedure – what you expect them to do.
How you expect the pupils to behave in order to be successful in the activity.

An exemplar set of instructions for giving your pupils a test is offered below:

1. Explain the rationale for your instructions

Explain to the pupils the benefits of following your instructions carefully.

On Friday you will have a test. At the beginning of the lesson I will give you instructions. It is very important that you follow these instructions carefully so that you complete the test and do well.

2. Involve pupils by asking questions

Pupils will follow your instructions more readily if you involve them in a discussion that rationally addresses their concerns.

What would happen if we wasted a lot of time getting ready for the test? What are the consequences of pupils not coming to the lesson with the correct equipment?

3. Explain the specific instructions for the test

Now teach the specific instructions that they will be expected to follow. Remind them that when everyone follows these instructions all pupils will have an opportunity to succeed in class.

I want you to clear your desks, except for a pen.

There is to be no talking or getting out of your seat.

When you receive your paper lay it face down on the desk until I tell you to begin.

When I say 'begin', turn your paper right side up, write your name and date, read the questions carefully.

When you are ready, begin writing.

If you have any questions put your hand up and wait until I get to you.

When you have finished, check over your answers, come to the front of the class and hand your sheet in. You may take out a book and read quietly until the papers are collected.

Again, I should like to return to the notion of 'control by anticipation'. In other words, it's a bit like Murphy's Law – if things can go wrong, they will. Clear, structured and well-thought-out instructions will go a long way to reducing the possibility of things going awry in your lessons. I am sure that some of you will greatly empathize with some of the examples given below of where instructions have been hurried and ambiguous and where things have not really gone according to plan.

NQT English

Year 7 love to ask questions and the majority of the time it drives me crazy! I can handle the occasional 'What's your middle name?' or 'Have you got a cat?', but the other day I set them a piece of work, blurted out what I wanted them to do and left them to it. Within seconds, the lesson had turned into chaos and all I could hear was 'I don't understand', 'This is crap', and 'What do we have to do?'. I wished I could have stayed calm and instructed them again, but if the truth be known, I didn't have a clue myself! This was due to having to do 160 reports and therefore letting my lesson planning go out of the window!

'Giving instructions to pupils is not as easy as it looks.'

NQT Science

I was getting pupils to do an experiment on lenses and focusing lengths. This was a high-ability class, so I gave verbal instructions and then asked if they all understood. They agreed, so I let them start. Within five minutes I had to get them to stop and show them a demonstration as no-one had the right idea. A very silly mistake! Next time, I will always do a demonstration and get them to repeat the set-up.

NQT English

The worst incidents, where instructions fail to be carried out successfully, are when you are ill-prepared and give instructions for a task which is yet to materialise in your head! You don't really know what you want the pupils to achieve and therefore, there isn't a remote chance that they will know what to do! You just feel like running away!

NQT PE

In PE there is a high risk of accidents or incidents because of the nature of the subject. It is important to have every pupil still and listening. On this particular occasion, I was trying to go through some recapped teaching points and said to the pupils, 'Can you hold your balls still!'. This may be fairly humorous, but can instantly change the mood and atmosphere. Pupils move from a state of concentration and focus to being silly and immature. It can be so difficult to refocus the pupils after such a slip of the tongue.

Body language, voice techniques and class control

There is a feeling among many teachers that the level of control and authority over their pupils has been severely eroded over the past 20 years. They feel that, in reality, there is very little they can really do should pupils decide to call their bluff. If this really is the case, then surely is it not the same for all teachers? Why is it then, that pupils take some teachers seriously but do not even give others the time of day? What is it about some teachers that causes them to have less grief with their classes than do other members of staff? To my mind teaching has a great deal in common with the theatre, with the good teacher taking on the role of the playwright, actor and critic. Successful teachers are those who have realized the need for them to utilize every aspect of their professional repertoire and to fully capitalize upon the actor in them to deal with everyday school situations.

Your body language

I have often been told by many pupils that I must have eyes in the back of my head but the simple reality is that I try to maintain a readiness for what could possibly go awry in my lessons. In almost expecting pupils to try it on, I am constantly aware of the types of misbehaviour likely to occur. In order to project this image I try to create an imposing and upright body posture to give an impression of being in control and to allow me to oversee the actions of the pupils in my classes. As it is important to give off an air of confidence and yet not appear to be defensive, I try to make sure that my arms are down by my sides and not folded across my chest.

Posture

Strong signals are given by our body posture and it is worth noting one or two tricks of the trade as far as using posture as a means of gaining control. There is relative power to sitting or standing. In school, where pupils are usually required to remain seated, it is powerful to stand next to someone who is sitting. You are much taller than the seated person and it is usually regarded as submissive to be lower. Any sociologist will tell you about the importance of power symbols in a classroom. A simple thing like seeing the caretaker and getting a large teacher's chair for your room can go a long way to giving off a symbolic message of the balance of power in your room.

On the level

Having just mentioned the importance of using your body language to distance yourself from the pupils, I am now going to offer you an alternative strategy. On occasions, one of the best forms of pupil control is to manipulate a situation where you almost become one of them. There are occasions where you can find the opportunity to sit with your pupils. This has much more the feel of equality and the pupils are then able to deal directly with you. Turning your whole body to face the person being addressed makes a conversation seem more personal. It also shows that you are prepared to be fully attentive and ready to share rather than to dominate. The irony is that it is this sharing experience with the pupils that provides a highly effective form of control when used wisely. The bottom line is that you

'In school, where pupils are usually required to remain seated, it is powerful to stand next to someone who is sitting.'

need to be aware of both types of control method and use them accordingly.

Eye contact

In my current position as Professional Development Tutor, I observe a whole range of staff. One of the main foci for these observations is classroom organization, management and discipline. As expected, things don't always go according to plan for these teachers in their lessons. At the beginning of each year I make presentations on the importance of using tactical control in the classroom. In particular, I regularly extol the virtues of both initiating, and maintaining, good routines in the classroom. It is fair to say that at the beginning of the year these members of staff do go through the ritual of setting up their expectations and outlining their ground rules, all the things I have asked them to do. So what exactly is missing? Why do the pupils not co-operate? What gave these teachers away was their reluctance to make full eye contact with the pupils whilst they were setting up routines. Why is eye contact so important? Apart from the obvious need to scan the class consistently for signs of pupils becoming distracted and veering off task, there is a need to use eye contact to involve all pupils in your lessons fully. Looking at a pupil in an interested and relaxed manner makes the conversation personal and fully involves them in what is going on in the lesson. It is almost like a 'psychological contract' that becomes very hard for the pupil to break. Haven't most of us been socialized into believing it to be rude to look away when someone is making eye contact with you? The eyes betray your confidence levels. The pupils can see in your eyes how secure and confident you feel. It is absolutely vital that, no matter how you actually feel inside, that you have the bottle to bluff it out when necessary.

The following quote from a Year 8 pupil about one of his teachers emphasizes the importance of eye contact in motivating and controlling pupils.

The way she conducted the lesson with such ease but so much enthusiasm and she looks her eyes with everyone's and walked in between our desks involving all pupils.

(Author's own BA research findings)

The voice

Your voice, along with a positive body stance and use of eye contact, is a very important tool of social control. So many people feel that shouting at pupils is the only way to convey your displeasure and to turn things around. I would be a hypocrite if I said that I didn't shout at pupils. I do, but I try to limit these instances to the times when I really need to make a point quickly. Shouting should generally be avoided because it tends to mean that the person shouting is not in control of the situation. However, on the other hand, a voice that is too quiet will be seen as non-assertive and could mean that no-one takes any notice of you. Try to maintain a well-modulated, confident voice tone when talking to pupils. I appreciate that this is not always easy,

'What gave these teachers away was their reluctance to make full eye contact with the pupils whilst they were setting up routines.'

especially when in fact that is the last thing you are feeling inside. If you are making a transition from one part of the lesson to another, then you need to alter your voice tone to indicate this. In order to establish your high expectations you need to use a strong assertive tone for setting up pupil assignments. Uncomfortable as it may be, it might be an idea to audio tape your lessons in order to try to ascertain the effect your voice is likely to have.

The following quote from another Year 8 pupil about one of their teachers illustrates the importance of voice tone in motivation and control.

A teacher should have different tones of voice to make things exciting and also interesting so that you don't fall asleep with boredom in the class. My English teacher from Year 7 sounded exciting when explaining a piece of work, also when reading to the class.

(Author's own BA research findings)

Gesture

Gestures accentuate what you are trying to say. Uninhibited movements tend to suggest openness and self-confidence but these should not be erratic and therefore give you the appearance of being nervous. The right hand gestures can add emphasis to your teaching points and go a long way to involving your audience in the proceedings. For example, drawing your hands towards your body can convey both warmth and your wish to involve all your pupils into the discussion. You can convey openness by sitting with your hands and legs uncrossed, by leaning forward and moving closer.

'Don't ever underestimate the importance of a smile.'

Don't ever underestimate the importance of a smile. You can convey sincerity if you smile, maintain long and positive eye contact and have open hands. Obviously you will give off a totally different message if you adopt a converse gesture. You will give a totally defensive impression if you purse your lips, avoid making eye contact, lean away and/or clench your fists.

In my opinion the biggest experts as to what makes a good teacher are the pupils themselves. You have already seen what a couple of pupils feel about this issue. The following quotes come from a range of Year 8 pupils during some classroom research on body language and effective teaching (from author's BA research findings).

A good teacher stands tall and confident when he is telling you things, which make him seem in control with power. When he talks to you he looks straight into your eyes making the message he's trying to get across become more strong.

A good teacher will stand up straight and walk around to be in control and confident that they can talk in front of a class. Also, they can look around at each pupil to show that 'I am here so nobody mess with me'. The voice can be nice so that they know the teacher is nice but go lower to say 'I don't want any messing around'. Facial wise if you are bad they give you 'evils' for a few seconds.

A good teacher I have stands in the middle of the class. He stands confidently and this makes him look more in control because he is bigger than the rest of the class. He keeps eye contact with a lot of the class and that looks like he means business and wants to teach rather than just make money. If someone talks in his class or forgets his homework, he shouts at them and gives them an extremely angry look. This keeps very good control of the class. His voice is loud and confident so that pupils know he means business. Teachers with weaker voices seem less confident so pupils are more disruptive.

My teacher uses lots of gestures to explain the work and points when he is telling someone off. This also keeps good control.

When this teacher teaches our class, he stands in the middle of the front of the class. This gives off the message that he is confident. He always stands tall and confidently. He mainly looks at the whole class but sometimes he looks at individual people to see if what he said has got through or not. You can tell he means business because his eyes open more.

A good teacher is someone who stands not sits because they're showing that they are getting involved with the class. Also a good teacher is someone who keeps their head up and looks at you instead of not looking at you the whole time in class. The teacher's facial expressions are important because if you do something bad you will know because of the way they look at you. The voice is important because you can tell if they mean business by the tone.

A good teacher will stand up when you're coming into the lesson to show you that they are ready to teach. When they are talking to the whole class they would try to stand in the middle of the class to try and get everybody involved and they will try and show everybody some eye contact. When they are teaching you separately they will give you eye contact. If they are in a big stress they will stare at you hard and give you the evils. They have to talk like they can be bothered. They should also use hand gestures to help things and to show how things are done. Also for posture they have to stand proud and big!

A good teacher is someone whose voice is in different levels such as high and cheerful and enthusiastic.

I am sure you will agree that the comments of these 13-year-olds are remarkably perceptive. True, the responses were preceded by a brief explanation by me as to exactly what was meant by terms such as 'gestures', 'posture', 'body language', etc., but the rest was down to them.

Whether you agree with it or not, we live in a consumer age and many educational pundits would suggest that teachers are being placed more and more in the market place. We have already seen in Section 1 how important first impressions are to youngsters. Perhaps the advice provided above will go some way to making that early good impression with your new classes.

'Don't ignore quiet pupils and don't allow individuals to dominate.'

2

The Role of Questioning
as a Classroom Management Tool

Establishing a collaborative climate

Have you ever attended a lecture or a meeting where you have simply been talked at for the duration of the session? Let's face it, if you do not feel involved in a project you tend to simply switch off. Youngsters are no different. When this happens, however, they are far less prone to adopt the passive role often taken up by adults in these situations, and are far more likely to make their feelings about things felt. Obviously this is where the disruptive behaviour comes into play. You *can* do something about this! In an earlier section we explored the need to use body language, eye contact and voice tone to make sure pupils feel involved. Now let's take that a stage further and explore the role of questioning in the classroom management equation.

It is vital that you involve as many pupils as possible in your question/answer and discussion sessions. Giving pupils a high degree of ownership of the lesson will have significant positive effects on your class control. Make sure you obtain a gender balance when choosing pupils to answer your questions. Don't ignore quiet pupils and don't allow individuals to dominate. Have a word with them privately, thank them for their enthusiasm and commitment, and explain to them the need to let others have a go. Much research has been carried out to show that a good questioning technique is at the heart of effective classroom control.

I am sure that you've all been there – you're in the process of conducting a class discussion or question/answer session with pupils in your class. It is difficult to keep some of the more dominant youngsters quiet but there are, nevertheless, a substantial number of pupils who fail to make much of a verbal contribution to lessons. These are the very youngsters who are going to become distracted and miss out on the learning experience. Why does this happen? It's not all down to the ability levels of the pupils involved. A lot of the time it is the brighter pupils who find it the most difficult to speak up in class. My experience of 'pupil watching', together with conversations with both parents and children, suggest to me that there are three main reasons for this.

The first cause relates to the pupils' perception of the value of actually participating verbally in class in the first place. Why should a pupil who is plodding along nicely, or who is already getting excellent grades in his/her written work, put themselves on the line by volunteering answers in class? The value of such a contribution needs to be made clear to them. Second, even some of the most able of pupils suffer from a crisis of confidence when it comes to speaking out in class. They're afraid of getting things wrong and making fools of themselves in front of their peers. They tend to ignore the fact that they are usually highly successful in their responses. Many pupils also hold back for fear of being labelled 'boffs' by their peers. The important thing to remember here is that it is their

'A lot of the time it is the brighter pupils who find it the most difficult to speak up in class.'

perception of the situation that affects their behaviour and which ultimately hinders their verbal contribution to lessons. They perceive the working culture of the classroom to be focused on the individual and to be competitive and threatening. This then leads them to opt out of the lesson and to subsequently become prone to distraction and misbehaviour. Third, a large number of pupils feel that they have no vested interest in what goes on in the classroom. Why should they get involved? This is something that an inclusive questioning technique can help to rectify.

If you are going to get all your pupils fully involved then you need to address these perceptions by creating a more collaborative and non-threatening climate within the classroom. I constantly tell my pupils that I am their 'safety blanket' and that they are to take risks in my classroom. If they fall I will catch them. A wrong answer in class should not invite ridicule, nor be dismissed by staff or fellow pupils, but should be seen as an important step in the journey towards achieving the objectives of that specific lesson. I have put together a number of strategies that I have found to work and which have gone a long way to producing a more collaborative atmosphere in the classroom. These strategies are not prescriptive. Take from them what you find useful. It is hoped that my ideas will provoke your own thought processes on the issue and that you will be able to devise your own methods for encouraging youngsters to participate more freely in class discussions in the future.

Some strategies for increasing collaborative learning in lessons

Getting the pupils to see the value of verbal participation in class

I feel that it is vital that pupils understand the value of making a verbal contribution to their learning. The processes of absorbing information from written or verbal stimuli, of synthesizing this material, of formulating a hypothesis and then of organizing one's thoughts into a coherent language form, provides ownership of the concept/issue being addressed and fully commits the pupil to the learning process. If this process does not take place, then a pupil is able to opt out too easily, is less likely to commit information/concepts to memory and is therefore unlikely to gain ownership of the material covered within the lesson. The rationale and importance of verbal participation in lessons by pupils should be established by teachers in their initial launch sessions with classes, and should be constantly reinforced by them throughout the academic year. The above process needs to be translated into a language that pupils will understand. I use the diagram in Figure 2 when trying to explain this process to the pupils in my class.

The building block model

The need for a collaborative approach to class discussions and question/answer sessions has already been outlined. What I felt was required, however, was a

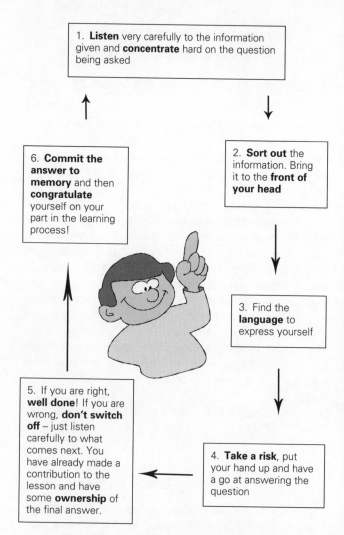

1. **Listen** very carefully to the information given and **concentrate** hard on the question being asked

2. **Sort out** the information. Bring it to the **front of your head**

3. Find the **language** to express yourself

4. **Take a risk**, put your hand up and have a go at answering the question

5. If you are right, **well done**! If you are wrong, **don't switch off** – just listen carefully to what comes next. You have already made a contribution to the lesson and have some **ownership** of the final answer.

6. **Commit the answer to memory** and then **congratulate** yourself on your part in the learning process!

Figure 2. The value of verbal contribution.

visual model that could be used to demonstrate this process to the pupils in my classes. I find that by using a set of wooden building blocks I am able to successfully get over the concept and value of collaborative learning in my class discussions and question and answer sessions.

At the beginning of the year I explain to the pupils that each wrong answer given in class acts as a stimulus (or building block) for another pupil to take on the thought process that little bit further. A wrong answer, therefore, is given a degree of status! A partially-correct response also brings us a little closer to that required answer (as shown in Figure 3) and, it too, acts as a building block for other pupils to further develop their thought patterns. Eventually, the correct answer is arrived at. I emphasize that the process is to be seen

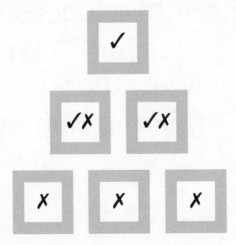

Figure 3. Building blocks towards a correct answer.

'I explain to the pupils that each wrong answer given in class acts as a stimulus for another pupil to take on the thought process that little bit further. A wrong answer, therefore, is given a degree of status!'

as collaborative and not individualistic. I have a poster on the wall that reinforces the view that it is 'OK to be wrong' and I try to point out that, without this full-class contribution, real learning then becomes the property of only the minority of pupils in the class. The other obvious correlation of successfully increasing pupil ownership of the lesson, is the dramatic decrease in discipline moves in lessons. I remember a HMI (Her Majesty's Inspector) saying to me after an OFSTED inspection – 'your pupils simply didn't have time to get distracted. They didn't know when they were going to be hit with a question next.'

Changing the culture

Don't expect miracles! Things won't change overnight. The pupils are going to need time to come round to the fact that you actually mean what you say about collaborative learning. You are, therefore, going to need some contingency strategies to bring about whole-class participation in oral work sessions. Below are a few ideas that I use to persuade, cajole and, ultimately, coerce pupils to participate in lessons.

If you know that the lesson is going to be dominated by oral work, give your questions a currency. Tell the class that you expect every pupil to answer a question during the lesson but that the earlier questions are going to be that little bit easier. By doing this, the more reluctant and/or less able pupils are more likely to respond in the early part of the lesson.

Taking the currency idea a stage further, try limiting each pupil to one answer during your question/answer session. Each pupil has then got to think very carefully what they spend their answer on. You need to advise the more able to wait until they receive the more challenging questions.

Before you start the lesson, explain to the class that you will be asking a specified number of pupils a question each on the content of your discourse. This usually has the required effect of gaining their full attention during that all-important launching period of the lesson. It thus provides an excellent tool for testing comprehension.

Use a process of elimination by asking pupils to put up their hands if they have not answered a question. Then, simply target your questions to the appropriate pupils in the class. Try to involve all the pupils.

Use a random method of questioning. Use two packs of cards. Give out one card per pupil. Put the remaining cards from both packs aside. Simply choose a card and ask the pupil with the corresponding card to answer your question. It's a bit of fun but gives the session a degree of 'tension' and keeps the pupils on their toes.

In mixed ability groups, where some less successful pupils feel reluctant to participate in front of their more articulate peers, it is important to adopt a strategy to keep them 'involved' and valued. Target specific questions at these pupils, but ensure they are of a low-level nature. Hopefully, a correct answer will be forthcoming (or at least a response which may provide a starting point for further discussion). Praise can be offered, especially when the answer creates an opportunity to build more blocks. The less able will have been seen to have participated successfully in the session by others in the class, and are more likely to feel good about themselves.

It is absolutely vital that you recognize the verbal contribution of those pupils in your classes especially those who usually cannot be bothered to, or those who do not find it easy to, participate. After all, it takes a lot of courage for some pupils to speak up in class. A quick word of praise, a telephone call home or the issuing of a community credit (a merit mark/sticker/stamp for positive actions within the class or school community) are just some of the ways their contributions can be acknowledged. Discuss the issue with individual pupils and set them targets. If possible, take the opportunity to discuss these with their form teachers. Let the pupils know that what you are asking them to do in class should be transferable across the curriculum i.e. what they can do in your lesson, they can do in others.

Questioning technique and use of wait-time

Many experienced teachers would admit that when they start teaching their new classes in September, they experience a degree of nervousness when standing in front of their pupils. I have spoken to colleagues who have also admitted, that, in their early lessons with their new pupils, they tend to rush proceedings. Because of the novelty of the situation, and because they don't know the pupils very well, there is a degree of tension in their question/answer session technique. Questions are rushed and pupils are not given enough time to think about their responses. Multiply this teaching behaviour by a factor of ten and we can begin to understand how inexperienced teachers may feel when confronted by new classes. It is this lack of confidence and nervousness that plays a large part in promoting misbehaviour and indiscipline in the classroom. If only we all had the courage and the confidence to bluff it out and to take things a little more slowly instead of trying madly to get through the lesson content as fast as we can.

My interest in the field of questioning as a means of pupil control has led me to explore the notion of wait-time. Over the past 20 years in contexts ranging from infant classes right up to university level, the concept of

'Many experienced teachers would admit that when they start teaching their new classes in September, they experience a degree of nervousness when standing in front of their pupils.'

wait-time has been explored. What exactly is wait-time and why is it important? It would seem from the research that a large number of teachers typically wait one second or less after they ask questions of their pupils, and that, after the pupils respond, they begin another verbal response in less than a second. According to Zimpher and Howey (1987), when teachers wait that extra three seconds or so, a number of effects are achieved including the following:

♦ the length of pupil responses increases between 300 and 400 per cent

♦ pupils are more prepared to support their answers with evidence

♦ pupils answer more questions in class

♦ pupils talk to other pupils about their work more

♦ failures by pupils to respond decrease

♦ the number of pupils voluntarily participating increases

♦ teacher discipline moves decrease .

The implications for pupil discipline are obvious. If they:

♦ respond more in these question/answer sessions

♦ work out a rationale for their responses

♦ ask more questions

♦ talk to their peers more about the work

♦ participate more fully in lessons.

Pupils are less likely to become distracted and become behaviour problems.

So, what are the implications for the teacher? Basically, if you can summon up the confidence to wait those extra two/three seconds before moving on to your next question you will reap the rewards of having a more involved set of pupils.

I hope that the strategies discussed above will go some way to illustrating the importance of fully involving your pupils verbally in lessons. What is evident from my research, is that full pupil involvement in lessons brings about a dramatic decline in discipline moves and is one of the most effective method of class control in a teacher's repertoire.

'In a busy teaching schedule, you cannot personally be expected to physically change the layout of the classroom for each type of lesson.'

3

The Importance of the Physical Environment

I have long held the belief that teachers, either wittingly or unwittingly, impose their personalities on their teaching bases. This can be for better or worse. A bright stimulating and well-organized classroom can go a long way to creating an effective learning environment. Conversely, a dull disorganized classroom creates a negative working ethos among the pupils.

Anyone who has any understanding of the power of the hidden curriculum will know that the physical environment of a school can have a dramatic effect on the quality of learning and teaching that goes on within it. The way a classroom is laid out, the quality of pupil display, the general condition and tidiness of the room all play a part in conveying positive or negative messages to the pupils about your expectations. The big question, therefore, is what does your classroom say about you?

When you are planning the layout of your classroom you need to give some thought to the ease of movement of your pupils within the room. You need to think about creating 'flow lines' in your classroom. Try to organize your furniture in such a way as to provide channels for easy pupil movement and to produce a feeling of space within your room. Before you set about doing this you need to ask yourself a number of important questions:

♦ Can your pupils make their way to their places without making physical contact with other pupils or their property?

♦ Can the pupils access the resources in your room easily?

♦ Have you placed difficult pupils near to your resource store?

♦ Can you wheel additional equipment such as video players, slide projectors, etc. into the room without having to get the pupils to move?

As classroom teachers we are all aware of the conflict that can occur when even unintentional physical contact is made between pupils during the course of a lesson. With a little bit of forethought many of these minor distractions can be avoided and the lesson is likely to run much more smoothly.

There has been much research to show the importance of routinization as an excellent way of establishing good classroom control and discipline. Your pupils should learn very quickly where all the resources for the lesson can be found. To this effect doing something as simple as labelling your resource drawers can save you a great deal of hassle during your lessons. How many times are you interrupted in lessons by pupils who say 'where is the lined paper, sir?' or 'where do you keep the coloured pencils miss?'. You then have to break off from what you are doing to deal with these questions. Setting up routines whereby pupils get to

The Importance of the Physical Environment

know where all the resources are, how to collect them and where to put them back are vital to the whole flow of the lesson. I have observed teachers, having gained the full attention and interest of all the pupils in the class, then having to break the flow of the lesson by asking pupils to go and collect the resources. Having resources already laid out on desks or ready to be collected by pupils when they come into the room can go a long way to alleviating many low-level discipline issues. So, how accessible do you make your classroom resources to your pupils?

Your classroom really is your 'pride and joy'. Pupils' work should be displayed on the walls in an effective and colourful manner. If you are not artistically or graphically oriented then seek advice from the Art or Technology Department. Make sure that you change pupil display regularly ensuring that you are showing examples of work from a range of ability levels. Why do I feel this is important?

Celebrating pupil success is a way of identifying exemplary practice for other pupils to learn from, but it is far more than this. Again, it is very much about increasing the level of pupil involvement and helping to reduce the marginalization of some of the youngsters in your classes. Chase up on any graffiti or vandalism in your room. In Section 1 we looked at the issue of establishing behaviours and expectations. If you do not follow up on a single act of graffiti, or at the very least, fail to show your disapproval, you are going a long way to establishing the notion that this behaviour is acceptable in your classroom. Once you get a reputation for following up on these types of behaviours, you will have very little trouble:

Managing Your Classroom

♦ Use your classroom to get your values across to the youngsters.

♦ Display the school and class rules on the notice board, put your visual versions of your rules and routines up on the wall.

♦ Take the opportunity to display advice and guidance about the way you want pupils to work in your lessons.

Again, we are back to the importance of the hidden curriculum in establishing the norms, values and skills required in your teaching area:

♦ How much attention do you give to the layout of your desks?

♦ Is the layout appropriate for the activity being undertaken?

♦ Do pupils get too socially comfortable in your classes?

♦ How often do you change your desk layout?

The desk layout for group work, for example, where you want lots of pupil interaction, is not appropriate when you want pupils to work quietly or on paired tasks. In a busy teaching schedule, you cannot personally be expected to physically change the layout of the classroom for each type of lesson. What you could do, however, is to draw up a number of layout permutations, say plan A, plan B and plan C, which can then be used by your appointed monitors to lay out the desks for you at appropriate times during the week:

The Importance of the Physical Environment

♦ How sure are you that your pupils can see the black/
  whiteboard or the video, or hear the audio tape
  easily from their positions in the classroom.

♦ Does the light from the window obscure the picture
  on the TV screen for example?

♦ Does the overhead projector itself obscure the view
  of the whiteboard for some pupils?

You need to constantly check this out with your
pupils as, and when, you change your furniture arrangements during the term. All of this contributes to a lack
of flow in lessons and gives the pupils opportunities to
become distracted or to distract others.

See again what the pupils have to say about the
importance of the physical environment in the learning
and teaching equation.

With the exception of one Year 11 lesson per week, I
am one of those teachers fortunate enough to have my
own teaching base. Two years ago, for timetable
reasons I was asked to teach one of these lessons in
another classroom. I very quickly became aware, however, that the quality of teaching and learning in the one
lesson conducted in the foreign classroom, was well
below that normally found in my own teaching room. I
was interested in finding out whether the pupils themselves would pick up on the cultures of the two different classrooms and how this perception would affect
their attitude, behaviour and motivation. These questions formed the basis of some low-level classroom
research. Should you be interested in finding out
more about the rationale and methodology of this
research, you will need to follow up on the article that

explores the impact of the 'physical environment' of a classroom on the behaviour of its pupils (Dixie, 2000).

It is necessary for me to briefly describe the classroom environment in which this Year 11 class had one of its lessons. The desks were positioned in rows facing a small whiteboard at the front of the class. This whiteboard was not big enough to project slides or OHT images on but could be used to write down assignment instructions. The blackboard and larger projection screen were situated at the back of the room, which effectively meant that pupils had to turn their chairs round if these teaching aids were to be utilized. Plug-point access could only be found for the television/video packages at the front of the room. Combined use of blackboard, OHT or slide projection screen could not therefore occur, since there was only one double socket with no adapters provided. Although experienced, the host teacher was an extremely busy member of staff and often did not find time to clear up her teaching desk. This caused difficulty when trying to find room to organize text books and resources for their effective distribution to the pupils.

It was in this context that the research was carried out. I selected a number of pupils and asked them each to complete a questionnaire. I explained to them that, although I would welcome responses to the specific questions being asked, I would also value their opinions on any issues relevant to the research enquiry. The findings were as follow:

Seven out of the eight respondents felt that the quality of teaching and learning was noticeably worse in the host classroom than in their normal geography room. According to them, much of this was down to not being aware of where the basic equipment in the room was kept. A number of them mentioned the resultant inconvenience that this causes, both to them and to me, during the lesson. One pupil wrote about this 'interrupting the flow' of the lesson and about me becoming 'edgy' when I was not able to find what I was looking for. Two pupils wrote about me becoming more 'stressed' when looking for equipment, when seeking space to place my resources or when trying to find a suitable place to put my overhead projector. One went on to say that this tension had a marked negative effect on the quality of teacher/pupil relationships in the class. She explained that the loss of time taken up in setting up this new room for the lesson meant that the pupils lost out on the individual attention they received in their 'normal' geography room. This view was supported by another pupil who went on to say:

'Make the most of your classroom as a creative base for good teaching and learning.'

The Importance of the Physical Environment

> We feel we can get away with more as there is a different atmosphere and your concentration is more on getting resources rather than on the individual pupils.

She then went on to write about the layout of the host classroom as being 'cramped'. And then offered the following description of her normal geography room:

> We are familiar with our original room and I find that it is more spaced out and has a better working atmosphere. We also have our resources where we know so we don't have to spend time looking or having to go and get the resources.

Tip

All of the respondents felt that, to some degree, the move had a negative effect on their motivation and behaviour. Two pupils wrote about it being more like a cover lesson rather than a normal geography lesson. They described their behaviour as being more unsettled in the host classroom, as opposed to their normal geography room. They both admitted to being more noisy, more prone to distraction and getting less work done. Another pupil wrote about the negative effect of the changed atmosphere on the behaviour and motivation of the pupils in the class.

Managing Your Classroom

Another pupil offered the following observation:

> I think the behaviour and motivation of the pupils is different for the worse, but I don't know why. The behaviour doesn't dramatically change but I notice a difference. I think that getting distracted is very easy but I don't know why. I don't think we get as much work done as in our normal teaching room because in our classroom the work environment is brighter and more spatial, whereas in the host classroom we are more cramped and we don't know where anything is.

Tip

Pupils in the survey wrote about me becoming edgy when unable to find the required resources in the host classroom, or when being constantly interrupted by pupils asking where equipment could be found. It is vital that pupils are routinized into knowing where text books, stationery, worksheets etc. are to be found and where they are to be returned to at the end of the lesson. They should also be routinized into making sure that rubbish is cleared away and into making sure that the classroom furniture is left in an orderly fashion before they leave the room.

The benefits of this are twofold; first you give less chance to the pupils to disrupt the flow of your lessons; second, you are then able to spend your time more constructively in welcoming the pupils to your next lesson instead of having to tidy up your classroom. The learning culture is, therefore, set up nicely for your next class.

So, what are the implications of these responses? The comments made by these pupils lend credence to my belief that the physical environment of a classroom can have a substantial effect on the attitudes, motivation and behaviour of the pupils within its confines. I continue to argue that a well-planned and well-organized classroom can provide a strong foundation for good order and discipline among the pupils in your charge. This view is supported by the pupils who responded to the questionnaire and whose highly perceptive comments lend weight to my argument. It is also supported by a number of colleagues who, despite being excellent practitioners, admit to having to work that bit harder to establish and maintain a positive ethos among their pupils in classrooms which are lacking in stimulus and which are devoid of good planning and organization.

Although there is very little we can do about the physical learning environment when we are forced to teach in alternative rooms, we can learn to appreciate the luxury of having our own teaching bases and do our best to make the most of this as a learning opportunity for the pupils.

The message is simple; make the most of your classroom as a creative base for good teaching and learning. Not everyone is fortunate enough to be blessed with a classroom they can call their own.

'Being late for lessons
is a very bad
management ploy.'

4

Gaining the Psychological Edge

Punctuality

How many times have you been in the following situation. You arrive late to a meeting only to find that everyone is already in the room, having already socially bonded, and already fully engrossed in the throes of working through the agenda. As you enter the room, you feel that everybody is staring at you and you begin to feel uncomfortable and embarrassed simply because you don't feel fully part of things.

In most professional situations this feeling doesn't last. Your colleagues usually do what they can to make you feel welcome and involved. Youngsters aren't always that generous. In that brief period before you arrive at your classroom, they have established a set of norms, a code of conduct and a high degree of social bonding which they are highly resistant to changing for what they 'perceive to be' an intruder. In other words, they have gained the psychological advantage.

Apart from being totally discourteous to the pupils, being late for lessons, is a very bad management ploy. Punctuality ensures that you are on 'home territory', that you are ready to meet the pupils on 'your terms' and that the psychological advantage is very much with you. If you are late to your lessons you will then have to spend valuable teaching time trying to wrest that psychological advantage back from your pupils. Why cause yourself these problems? However, in situations where teachers have to move from one classroom to another, lateness is bound to occur through no fault of their own. Pupils will definitely pick up on your discourtesy towards them if they know that you have simply been having another cup of coffee in the staff room, when you should have been making your way to their class. If you are late, then my advice would be to lead by example, and to apologize to the class giving your reasons for not being in the class when they arrived. This will make it a lot easier when it comes to dealing with pupils who come late to your lessons. Always challenge lateness in such a way which makes it obvious to the class that punctuality is important but do so in a way that does not cause an interruption to the flow of your lesson. Simply by telling the miscreants that you will be dealing with them later will get the message across to the class about your view on lateness. Once again, however, it is vital that you actually do follow this up and that you don't simply forget about the issue. Remember the important phrase 'certainty rather than severity'.

Get to know your pupils by name

Knowing your pupils by name is absolutely vital to good classroom control. You need to think seriously about the psychological advantage of getting to know a pupil's name and using it. Once a pupil has been addressed by his/her personal name they feel a sense of status and involvement – a bond is established and an informal contract has been forged.

This is the first stage in getting the pupils on your side and in making them feel special, which reduces the likelihood of them misbehaving in your class. There are a number of ways to learn pupils' names; you could sit them in class alphabetically until you have learned their names off by heart; you could take a class photograph and attach it to your register sheet; you could turn the process into a game, giving a small prize at the end of the lesson to those pupils you are unable to name.

Much social control is carried out simply because pupils like you. Smile as much as you can at pupils. A sense of humour is also vital: know when to laugh at yourself. Humour often diffuses a potentially difficult situation!

Take every opportunity at break times, along corridors, on field trips, on Activities Day, etc. to be friendly to pupils especially those who you have recently admonished for their inappropriate behaviour. Take this opportunity to build bridges. It will pay off in the classroom!

Think about the structure of your lessons

Often a lesson gets off to a bad start because pupils don't always arrive at the classroom at the same time. They may have to come from completely disparate parts of the school and it is important for you to think about catering for this occurrence. One of the best ways to get your pupils ready for the lesson is to set some kind of holding task. This could be in the form of a

'Much social control is carried out simply because pupils like you.'

teaser or a task that pupils have to do in the back of their books until you are ready to formally start the lesson. Apart from increasing pupil knowledge and providing them with more opportunities to improve their thinking skills, it can have a dramatic effect on behaviour and motivation in that early part of the lesson. In order to do this task, pupils have to get their equipment out of their bags, get their books out and generally get organized. If you make these holding tasks part of your lesson routines, you are less likely to have to nag them about getting themselves sorted out before the start of the lesson.

Any teacher who has been through the dreaded OFSTED process will know how much HMI stress the importance of sharing lesson objectives with their pupils. Inspection issues aside, I would certainly support doing this simply because it is good practice. However, I would go further than this. I feel it is absolutely vital to share the lesson journey with the pupils. An example of exactly what I mean by this is shown below.

Right – I am going to explain the objectives of this session and then I am going to tell you exactly what we are going to do at various times during the lesson. The journey is as follows:

♦ 0–5 minutes: I will outline the lesson objectives and we will then discuss these.
♦ 5–10 minutes: we will explore the resources and see how they match up with the lesson objectives.
♦ 10–25 minutes: you will have an 'active' group work.
♦ 25–35 minutes; we will discuss the results of your task.
♦ 35–55 minutes; you will complete a short written assignment.
♦ 55–60 minutes; we will discuss how the lesson objectives have been met.

Why is it important to break the lesson into time slots and why, more importantly, have I seen it necessary to inform the pupils of the structure of the lesson? You may have heard of the expression 'We live in a three-minute culture', inferring that people in our society today have short attention spans. Well, I wouldn't go quite, say, three minutes, but I certainly do believe that a lack of focus and concentration in lessons plays a major role in creating disruption in our classrooms today. Breaking the lesson down in varied and manageable time slots is more likely to stimulate the interest of the youngsters in our classes. I'm sure most of us do this as a matter of course. However, how many of us actually share the lesson journey with our pupils. Knowing that they only have to focus for, say, ten minutes, before they are going to make a transition to another activity, makes it easier and more worthwhile for an easily distracted pupil to focus and take on board what the teacher is saying. If the pupils perceive that they are going to have to sit still and listen for the whole lesson, they will switch off and you will find it difficult to get them re-focused when and if you do change the lesson activity.

Use praise effectively

Never underestimate the effect of praise as a behaviour management tool. Just think about how positively you have felt when someone has taken the time and trouble to say a big 'well done' to you. Most of us respond to praise positively and using it in the right way can dramatically increase motivation and achievement among your pupils. True, youngsters might not readily admit to it, but I am convinced that they relish praise along with the rest of us.

Remember that some adolescents do not respond well to praise given in front of their peers. With these pupils it is best to deliver praise quietly after class or unobtrusively during the lesson. Be very aware that you can often win over potential troublemakers by giving them the esteem they have failed to gain in other areas of their lives. Effective praise, however, must be genuine, descriptive and specific. It is important not to praise pupils unless you really mean it! Show that you are genuinely appreciative of their work ethic or of the appropriateness of their behaviour. Pupils need to know exactly what they are being praised for. By being specific about the behaviours you wish to credit them for, they are more likely to repeat the desired behaviour in the future. The following examples shows how you can use praise as a vehicle for classroom control:

Tom, I am really pleased to see you have worked quietly and not got out of your seat during this lesson.

Hannah, I have to say that the way you came into this room, got your books out and sat quietly waiting for me to start, was absolutely excellent. Well done.

You may be aware that, although the majority of pupils in your class may be behaving appropriately, there may be one or two pupils who are not carrying out your routines. You may find that using proximity praise provides an effective way of gaining class control. Rather than focusing negatively on the inappropriate behaviour of these pupils, simply praise those pupils who are behaving appropriately. Remember, once again, to be specific about the desired behaviour you wish to encourage. Proximity praise can also be used on a more individual level. An effective way to redirect a non-disruptive off-task pupil back on task is to focus on the appropriate behaviour of those pupils around him. The following is an example.

Tips

The entire class, with the exception of Michael, is working independently on their research reports. Rather than answering the questions, Michael is staring out of the window. On either side of Michael, Dawn and Maria are both doing their work. Wanting to get Michael on task, the teacher says, 'Dawn and Maria, you both look like you're really into this task. Well done!' As she expects, Michael looks around him, notices what is going on and gets back to work. The technique is doubly effective: off-task pupils are motivated to get back on task, and pupils who are on task receive well deserved praise.

Remember that praise does not necessarily have to be verbal. Letters sent home or use of the school credit system, can all have positive effects on pupil motivation and, consequently, on their behaviour in your teaching area. Although this institutional praise can go a long way to improve the motivation and behaviour of the pupils in a school, I feel it is the individual teacher's 'personal touch' that is the most effective motivational and behavioural tool. Getting your own rubber stamp with your own idiosyncratic message designed on it and using it to reward pupils for good work or behaviour, is a simple but highly effective classroom management tool.

A very simple but effective ploy to reward pupils is to put a comment in pupils' exercise books and get the Head of Year, Form Tutor and parents to put their signature, comments and date next to mine. By doing this, not only have you dramatically improved home–school relationships, but the pupils concerned receive praise from four quarters. Try it and notice the difference in their motivation and behaviour.

Creating tension in lessons

I mentioned in Section 1 the need for pupils to feel safe and secure in their lessons if real learning is going to take place. I explained that this was one of the prerequisites of the reptilian brain, that primeval part of the brain that helps us to function when threatened by physical, mental or emotional stress. However, things mustn't get too cosy! There's nothing like a small amount of healthy tension in classes just to keep pupils on their toes and in a state of readiness for learning. While the pupils are in this heightened state they are less likely to misbehave in lessons. It is amazingly simple to create this degree of tension in your classes. I have included a few ideas below.

Tips

During the establishment phase of the year ask the pupils for their home telephone numbers. This creates a degree of uncertainty among the pupils. I am in no doubt that someone will ask why you need them. Keep a wry smile on your face and tell them that you need their numbers so that you can contact their parents in the light of poor or exceptional work from them. Just a word of advice here. Never telephone home without the knowledge and permission of the Head of Year. They are likely to have a much greater knowledge of the home backgrounds of these pupils and of the context of their behaviour.

When launching the instructional phase of the lesson, pre-warn the class that you will be selecting, at random, the names of, say, five pupils to feed back your instructions to the rest of the class at the end of the session. The uncertainty of whether they are going to be the 'unlucky ones' who are to be picked on tends to bring about a sharper focus among the pupils.

Standing silently behind pupils who are not on task can also have a re-focusing effect on pupils and lets them know that 'you are on their case'.

A continued look of disapproval can also often do the trick. Have the courage to establish, and maintain, that all important eye contact and don't turn away until you are satisfied that the pupil has complied with your wishes.

Don't let the pupils get too comfortable and predictable in their seating patterns. Make name cards for your pupils and change the seating arrangements from time to time. When asked by the pupils why I have done this, I simply tell them that education is about more than just bookwork and examinations. It is about getting on with and working with all different types of people.

If you are not satisfied that a pupil is fully on task, simply write the time in the margin of their exercise book and then walk away. The implied consequence of this action is that some form of sanction will follow should the pupil concerned not increase their work rate before the end of the lesson.

Don't forget the importance of non-verbal communication as a means of creating tension and of gaining effective classroom control. We have already explored the power of the 'stare', but there is also a place for using hand signals to illustrate disapproval. The call of a pupil's name or a flat-hand 'halt' signal followed by a 'thumbs up' to indicate an assumption that the pupil will respond positively to your demand, is often enough to do the trick.

Scanning and circulating the classroom

Scanning is simply the art of having eyes in the back of your head. It is the ability to use your peripheral vision to check what is going on in your classroom while at the same time giving your attention to other pupils or tasks. This is useful when you are working with a small group of pupils and/or with individual pupils while the rest of the class is working independently. The objective of this technique is to reinforce pupils who are on task, thereby encouraging them to remain so. It will also help you to recognize pupils who may not normally receive attention until they misbehave. By using this method you can keep independent workers on task and still remain working with one small group. Here's how to use the scanning technique:

1. When you are working with a small group, look up every few minutes and scan the pupils who are working independently.

2. In situations where pupils are not working appropriately then give them a disapproving look, a hand signal, or have a quiet word with them.

3. When you notice pupils who are working appropriately, take a moment to recognize good behaviour. You could say something like, 'The group near the window has been working non-stop on this

assignment. Well done and thank you!' The pupils will appreciate the recognition and continue working independently. Other pupils will get the message that you are aware of what's going on in the room, and will be more motivated to stay on task themselves.

4. Occasionally you need to move away from your current position and circulate the room continuing to give positive recognition to those pupils on task. You can quietly and unobtrusively let a pupil know that you recognize his or her appropriate behaviour. Just make the odd positive comment about their work:

Jason, the first line of that speech will really grab the audience – well done.

Georgina, you have made excellent use of the key on your map – well done.

Use of the tactical pause and take up time

What do you do when, having scanned the classroom, you observe pupils who are not on task? I would fully support Rogers' (1998: 57) view that this is very much the time to use what he calls 'tactical pausing' and 'take up' time. This is a really effective way to increase attention when communicating an important message to your pupils. Use the pupil's name, then pause dramatically before going on to give them the instruction to get back to their work. It is that dramatic pause

'Use the pupil's name, then pause dramatically before going on to give them the instruction to get back to their work.'

that creates a degree of tension, which implicitly indicates your requirement that the pupil stops what he or she is doing and that he or she make full eye contact with you. It also provides an opportunity for take up time. Having gained the eye contact of the pupil and having made your point, you need turn away giving him/her time to carry out your demands in a dignified manner. Maintaining eye contact for too long in situations such as this tends to be confrontational and often brings about unacceptable secondary behaviour.

You will be amazed at how doing such a simple thing as this can lessen your need to wield the big stick in order to gain control over the pupils in your classes.

'Any teacher who has been through the dreaded OFSTED process will know how much HMI stress the importance of sharing lesson objectives with their pupils.'

5

Conclusion

Let's face it, we've all had personal battles with 'problem' pupils in our classes. Often these pupils have a tendency to act as catalysts for conflict in lessons, constantly stirring up trouble and friction among those around them. As far as you are concerned these young students undermine your authority as well as your confidence levels and seriously damage the learning of others. When they are absent from school I should imagine that you breathe a sigh of relief. For this small minority of youngsters, setting up an infra-structure based upon preventative discipline appears to be both irrelevant and ineffective.

You will go a long way to reducing general low-level disruption in your classes and this will give you more time to produce behaviour plans and to focus on those higher level discipline problems. It is also important that you do not beat yourself up if things don't always go according to plan. Even after 30 years of teaching, I come out of some lessons thinking to myself that that was an absolute shambles and that I was really glad I did not have an NQT observing the lesson. If you get things right 80 per cent of the time you are doing well. On its own, gaining proficiency in the use of tactical control is not enough. It is vital that you work hard at getting to know your pupils, at improving your relationships and at improving the level of your clinical

'Let's face it, we've all had personal battles with "problem" pupils in our classes.'

decisions. In short you need to become a fully fledged reflective practitioner.

'Even after 30 years of teaching, I come out of some lessons thinking to myself that that was an absolute shambles and that I was really glad I did not have an NQT observing the lesson.'

Bibliography

Dixie, G. (1998) 'Free speech', *First Appointments*, 19, *Times Education Supplement*.

Dixie, G. (2000) 'A room you can call your own', *First Appointments*, 20, *Times Education Supplement*.

Rogers, B. (1998) *You Know the Fair Rule*, London: Pitman.

Smith, R. (1996) *Develop Your Own Classroom Control and Discipline*, Lancaster, UK: Framework.

Wragg, T. (1995) 'Teachers' First Encounters with their Classes', in Moon, B. and Shelton, A. (eds) *Teaching and Learning in Secondary School*, London: Open University, pp. 114–24.

Zimpher, N. and Howey, K. (1987) Adapting Supervisory Practices to Different Orientations of Teaching Competence, *Journal of Curriculum and Supervision*, Winter (2), 104–7.

'Maintaining eye contact for too long in situations tends to be confrontational and often brings about unacceptable behaviour.'